Net Neut~~rality~~

And Why it Should Matter to Everyone

By June Sato

information contained within this document, including, but not limited to, —errors, omissions, or inaccuracies.

Table of Contents

Introduction

Talks and discussions on Net Neutrality are raging all over the globe. That is not surprising considering the fact that the Internet has become the playground for millions and millions of people in every nook and corner of the world. This amazing invention has opened doors of opportunity and learning that hitherto were thought non-existent or imaginary.

This book aims to throw some amount of clarity on this rather controversial topic. It deals with various questions about net neutrality ranging from the basic "what is net neutrality" or those with a more philosophical twist such as the ethics associated with the much-raged subject. So, I hope you enjoy reading the book as much as I enjoyed writing it.

Chapter One: Understanding Net Neutrality

Today, when you connect via the Internet, there are some expectations you have. For example, you expect to connect to any website you want to reach; you expect that your Internet Service Provider isn't discriminating information being streamed to you based on your choice of content or website, etc. In other words, you expect that you are in control of your Internet experience. That is to say, you want to enjoy the experience of net neutrality.

So, what is net neutrality? It is the most basic principle on which the power of the online communication through the Internet is kept sacrosanct. It is the Internet's guiding principle that aims to keep out lobbyists and greedy capitalists so that every human being is allowed to access the content he chooses without being unduly discriminated against.

A good analogy that can be used to define Net Neutrality is the concept of toll roads. There are multiple toll roads all over the US and multiple companies managing them. As a user, it doesn't matter which company is managing them because you get to travel through all the roads without feeling discriminated against because of being a member of one company or the other.

Net neutrality is the underlying guiding principle of the free Internet that ensures companies such as Comcast, AT&T, Verizon, etc. do not get the power to throttle data in a discriminatory fashion that will leave those who choose a different path at a difficult disadvantage. This was the way the Internet had always worked.

The architecture of the Internet is also designed to meet this basic guiding principle of allowing everyone to access data without discrimination. The architecture is so designed that information is transmitted across the Internet in standardized packets irrespective of what the content is or who the sender and/or the receiver is. This non-discriminatory architecture is central to the concept of Net Neutrality.

Moreover, the standardized packets enable the smooth movement of data without being impeded by the actual nature of the content. The primary reason behind the stupendous success of the Internet is this free-flowing data in a non-discriminatory fashion. The Net Neutrality guiding principle allows you to choose the content and websites you want to browse without any skewed and/or veiled compulsions and Internet offerings from your Internet Service Provider or anyone else.

What Happens When Net Neutrality Rule Is Abolished?

Without the Net Neutrality Rule in places, large and rich players such as Verizon, Comcast and AT&T will have the power to call all the shots associated with the Internet. They will be empowered to decide on which content or which application or which website you should access. In the absence of Net Neutrality Rules, it will be like your phone company deciding on things like who you should call or not call using their communication services.

Large Internet service providing companies will be legally empowered to slow down and/or hasten the speed of a particular content type or website or application which will result in them choosing which businesses should flourish and which should not flourish. Large Internet service providers will become legally empowered to offer preferential treatment to those companies that can afford to pay a higher cost while leaving out the open services of the Internet from benefitting those business entities which cannot afford the extra fees.

Except for those that can pay the exorbitant costs, others could be relegated to lower speeds of Internet access resulting in open and lawful discrimination. The absence of Net Neutrality will result in a situation in which the disadvantaged will feel like pariahs and outcasts in the Internet world as they are not rich or influential enough to afford the not-so-free Internet anymore.

The consequences of abolishing the Net Neutrality Rule is bound to have the most devastating effects on marginalized communities such as the LGBTs, the racial, religions, or other kinds of minorities, etc. who will not have much access to voice their discontentment and ire leading to strong communal issues. The human history is rife with horror stories of unresolved or even suppressed communal issues especially those associated with various kinds of minorities.

Importance of Net Neutrality for Racial Minorities

A free, open, and unbiased Internet offers a powerful platform for racial minorities to voice their concerns and fight against discrimination. The reason why activists are able to bring out a lot of people on to the streets to protest or to create awareness about their causes and their problems is that right now the Internet is designed in such a way that no individual or entity can throttle or control the movement of these messages through the Internet. Their ISPs are free to receive all kinds of messages and content.

Even otherwise, the media is highly dominated by the majorities, thanks to economic and other inequalities to racial minorities. Media control by the majority was the primary cause of dehumanizing and criminalizing racial minorities as their ideas and concerns were always suppressed or kept in the dark by the controlling party. The invention of the Internet was a highly positively turning point for these people.

Despite the majority dominance that is existent even today, the racial minority communities are able to garner support for causes and raise their voices against all kinds of injustices meted out to them through the free, open, and non-throttled Internet where data and information flow is not discriminated each other.

If Net Neutrality is lost, it is possible to use arm-twisting and/or cost-related elements to block out content and data from and to these ISPs leaving them in the dark again. Loss of Net Neutrality will result in the loss of an extremely important platform the racial minorities. Additionally, small businesses owned and managed by people from the racial minorities will also be hit by the loss of Net Neutrality.

Importance of Net Neutrality for Small Businesses

It is absolutely essential to have Net Neutrality for small businesses to survive and thrive in this wide, global market. With the absence of the Internet, small businesses will never be able to market their products and services and take them to every nook and corner of the world without fear of being overwhelmed by the logistical and marketing power of a large corporate house. Moreover, history is again rife with success stories in which a large part of the innovation happens as a small start-up, as a cottage industry, or in the garage of a home.

An open and free Internet is the basis for starting, sustaining, and growth of any startup. It is the foundation of innovation and creativity. Without a free Internet, small businesses will have to shut shop as they may never be able to spend huge amounts for marketing and reaching out to customers.

Internet Service Providers as gatekeepers to the Internet will be put in a position of immense and exploitative kind of power to call all the shots leaving everyone outside their realm at their mercy. Loss of Net Neutrality will destroy the level-playing field and fairness that is part and parcel of the Internet today.

After all, aren't Google, Facebook, etc the spectacular results of free and open Internet architecture? So, would it now be fair to keep the future generation in the dark and not give them the same platform to create another Google or Facebook?

Effects of Loss of Net Neutrality

The loss of Net Neutrality could lead to many problems for the common and some of the top issues can be broadly classified under three headings including increased costs, discrimination in accessing and flow of content, and considerable negative impact on innovation. Let us look at each in a bit of detail.

Increased Costs – If Net Neutrality is taken away, then it is possible that social media platforms like Twitter, Facebook, etc might start charging members for using and accessing social media content. Service Providers might begin to offer different packages at different costs. It is possible that if members cannot afford the cost of a particular tier then the media content will flow to them at much lower speeds preventing a smooth Internet experience. The person paying a lower cost might have to make do with slow streaming video or cannot have the same video game experience as the person who can afford the higher package cost.

Moreover, large online shopping companies like Amazon can bulldoze the market by paying large amounts to get preferred treatment so that their websites load at a faster rate. This will not only kill less dominant competitors but also take away the power of 'customer is king' as the customer will not be able to compare owing to far slower loading speeds of competing websites.

While the cost increase may not be possible to quantify right now, Portugal, which is a country without the Net Neutrality Rule can be used as an example to understand this element better. The most basic package offered by an Internet Service

Provider in that country is one that has only basic email services like Yahoo Mail and Gmail. Another package includes Netflix and YouTube also. A third one could include music apps such as SoundCloud, Spotify, Google Play Music. A fourth package comes with social media sites and other messaging apps like Skype, FaceTime, WhatsApp, etc. All these packages only include big names and leave out all small competition which is the third element of concern from throttling Net Neutrality.

Discrimination in Flow of Data – If Net Neutrality ceased to be, then there is a possibility by which service providers will offer fast lane data lines to people who pay more and slow lane data lines to those who don't pay. All websites and all content will not be treated in the same standard way.

Service providers who offer cable TV services might choose to send data coming from streaming video services like Netflix and Amazon so that they end up cross-selling their own products to their customers. The reason why YouTube is such a big hit is that there are no separate fast lanes that streamed video faster than what was offered by YouTube.

YouTube got the same treatment that Google or any other video streaming application got. The power and popularity of content raised the level of YouTube to where it is today. If Net Neutrality ceased to exist, new and upcoming video streaming founders will be at a disadvantage as the large players will flex resource muscles to keep out new and emerging competition.

Innovation Could Get Impacted Negatively – New and emerging companies will be hit badly as they will never be able to match the resources of large corporate giants. If the cost increases so much that it beats the economic purpose of new discoveries and innovation, then this aspect of the business is bound to suffer badly.

Service providers could levy excess tolls or use other measures to reduce access to their websites to consumers leading to both discouraging effects on innovation and reduced customer happiness. The customer is happiest when he gets plenty of options, isn't it?

Thus, net neutrality is bound to hit the common man and new innovations quite a bit and if this becomes a reality, the way Internet worked until now will change drastically.

I thought it best to clarify one little point of conflict that usually comes up in the Net Neutrality debate and that is between the concept of free and open Internet to one and all without discrimination and genuine traffic management techniques used by nearly all service providers. So, here goes a little subsection on that aspect of the Net Neutrality dialogue which is being discussed in the next chapter.

Chapter Two: Traffic Management and Net Neutrality

The Internet is today undoubtedly an indispensable tool that has taken over the day-to-day life in our planet. The Internet is the basic facilitator for both economic growth as well as innovation. The demand for Internet access with high-speed bandwidths is only going to grow further and there is very little chance for this demand to subside or even reduce.

In fact, even now, most Internet service providers and other network operators use different traffic management techniques to ensure users are not affected by huge and/or unprecedented during peak times. These traffic-management tactics are also causing concerns among people that network-operators can tweak elements in their system to deliver preferred treatment to any section of their leaving the others at a disadvantage.

Therefore, these traffic management practices have also come under the scrutiny of Net Neutrality observers as they believe intentional discrimination will jeopardize the basic principle of free Internet. Net Neutrality Rule ensures the availability and preservation of an open and free Internet which is a key element for it to remain a driver of growth, innovation, and free expression.

However, many times, using correct traffic management techniques could help in ensuring the Net Neutrality is maintained and everyone gets free and open access to the Internet. Yes, the debate is controversial and yet, good traffic management planning can be beneficial to one and all. For example, sensible traffic management techniques could protect and prioritize emergency-management calls over others. So, the question here is not whether traffic management is wrong but whether the approaches used are not infringing the Net Neutrality concept. Service providers usually manage traffic in two ways:

Best-Effort Access to the Internet - They use the 'best effort' principle of delivering data to all in more or less equal measure. This 'best effort' principle ensures that no one particular service or content type or application is given more or less importance over another. There is no manipulation of deliberate blocking or hinder to any particular website(s) or ISP(s).

Managed Services – Under this management technique, the network companies deliberately prioritize traffic. For example, a network service company might add more value to a video streaming service than it does to a mailing service resulting in deliberately managing traffic over the former. However, this method is not discriminatory at all and is used only to ensure overall efficiency of the network system.

Network services and the common people would benefit considerably if a sensible combination of the two measures is used effectively to manage traffic. To ensure transparency in the traffic management mechanism, many governments are passing rules by which service providers are mandated to document traffic management policies. Despite these regulations, traffic management techniques are constantly questioned and the challenges that are commonly discussed in the Net Neutrality dialogue include the following five items:

1. Filtering and Blocking
2. Internet Fast Lanes
3. Throttling
4. Zero-Rated Services
5. Market Competition

Filtering and Blocking

The filtering and blocking mechanisms are used by operators to deny users access to certain kinds of data. This is usually used to meet regulatory requirements or to meet certain business objectives that are clearly specified to the end users at the time of signing the membership agreement.

While some see filtering and blocking of content as ways of denying access to the completely free and open Internet, others view it as mandatory to either meet regulatory requirements or to keep minors and children safe from some kind of people and content. In fact, filtering and blocking of objectionable content is a mandatory regulatory requirement in many countries of the world.

Internet Fast Lanes – Internet operators could have agreements among themselves to provide faster speeds and preferential treatment to certain types of data based on business requirements. For example, video streaming businesses need a faster routing option to offer clients an optimum video viewing experience.

While some view this method as discriminatory, others see it as a necessity in order to provide better Internet experience to users. The latter group argues that if video streaming services are not given the seemingly preferential treatment over others, viewers are not going to be benefitted. Therefore, this side states, there is a need to manage traffic effectively so that end users (read: the average common citizens) are benefitted.

Throttling – This term is used to describe operators' methods to reduce information throughput rates from or to certain websites/content/application. Throttling mechanisms could include reducing the download and/or upload speeds of certain kinds of data. While some view this method as delivering preferential treatment against the norms of Net Neutrality, others view this as a necessity to avoid poor network performance and to avoid congestion.

Still others believe that these kinds of throttling mechanisms are unfair especially when the network operators are not transparent enough and disclosed openly to their members. They argue that lack of transparency is certain to lead to misuse of throttling mechanisms.

Zero-Rated Services – This term is used to describe a method by which network operators offer clients certain types of Internet access at zero or at negligible rates. These subsidies are usually exchanged for substantial and tangible market advantages including preferential access rights to deliver Internet services or an increased customer base or something else that usually puts competition at a huge disadvantage.

This method raises concerns in the minds of some people that it could lead to discrimination against content and data that are not offered under the zero-rated services. Yet others worry that if this is not offered, how will people who cannot afford any Internet services at all be provided with access to the Internet, no matter how seemingly discriminatory and/or if they receive only a small subset of the entire gamut of services.

This point is discussed prominently specifically in developing countries where many people cannot afford to pay for Internet access. The only way these people can be included is through zero-rated services, the proponents of this method argue.

Market Competition – Debaters for the cause of Net Neutrality argue that healthy market competition is critical to the growth of any market. If Net Neutrality didn't exist in markets that have few affordable options, the users there could become vulnerable to getting only restricted content and experiencing poor Internet quality.

Healthy competition is always good for customers as operators will vie with each other to provide better services at the same cost. This will be very beneficial to customers as they can have more options to choose from even as market players continuously work to improve service and lower costs.

Thus, every point of contention has issues from both sides of the Net Neutrality debate categorized under traffic management. It is imperative that as a mature civilization, we bring all elements to the table and sort out differences while ensuring the end users and all stakeholders are optimally benefitted.

Chapter Three: Arguments for and against Net Neutrality

The fundamental core of the Net Neutrality debate is who or what should control the flow of information over the Internet. Like everything else in this world, this debate too has people on both sides; those that argue for and those that argue against. The ones who argue for Net Neutrality will give you a perspective about its pros and those who argue against it will give you a perspective on its cons.

Without Net Neutrality, the service providers will have more control over the data as they can put huge caps and limitations on the usage of the Internet. This could lead to severe limitations placed on the common man and startups leaving larger advantages to the bigger players in the market.

Yet, service providers have their own problems and they have valid points in support of their claim to eliminate Net Neutrality. Let me use a simple example of water connections to explain the problem of Net Neutrality. Water supply companies like Internet service providers are utility companies which are a unique sort of business to own and manage.

It takes a lot of money to build network systems and pipes and tanks to connect all homes to the main water supply. But when you have one set of hardware in place, there is no need for another one to be put. For example, does your street have more than one water pipeline? Nor will it have more than one telephone pole.

The companies that build such systems naturally get a monopoly over the business because they own the hardware connecting the entire system. This could put consumers at huge risk. Take for example, what if one fine day, your water utility company chooses to quadruple rates. Where will common consumers go for water except to give in to this monopolistic attitude and actually be prepared to pay the unreasonable sum demanded?

To prevent such mishaps, even highly capitalized markets such as the United States, have regulations to keep in check potential unreasonable demands of utility companies. They are essential services that cost a lot of money to set up and yet they have to be heavily regulated. The regulation cannot be so stringent that nobody wants to do the job because the absence of a water supply line is worse than paying four times the amount for water, right?

Today, the Internet has become like an essential service and hence, people are asking themselves where it needs to be regulated or continue to be free as it is right now. While the proponents of Net Neutrality say yes, the opponents believe it should not be regulated and they should get a free hand to do what is best for their business.

Considering the sensitivity of the debate and the big stir that it is creating all over the world, I thought it made sense to include a chapter that laid bare both the advantages and disadvantages of Net Neutrality as proposed by the respective proponents.

Pros of Net Neutrality

Net Neutrality Keeps Costs Affordable – Companies like Netflix and Amazon Prime who cater to cord cutters are usually Net Neutrality supporters. Cord cutters themselves are big supporters of Net Neutrality. This is a natural expectation because, without Net Neutrality, the Internet service providers will target these companies only first because of their large bandwidth needs. Without the protection of Net Neutrality, Internet service providers will be free to penalize them for their bandwidth-guzzling activities.

So, without Net Neutrality, what is expected to happen? ISPs could have the power to bundle sites and sell them as packages. This will work exactly like how cable TV works in which your cable TV operator can choose to exclude HBO or MTV2 or any other channel unless you took a package which cost more. Similarly, your Internet service operator could 'block' out Netflix or Amazon Prime or YouTube.

Of course, this can be overcome if users are willing to take a hit on quality if the ISP only chooses to throttle video streaming channels instead of completely blocking it. However, another option could be that the video streaming channel is willing to pay more to get on the right side of the ISP who will then neither block nor throttle the particular channel. This is bound to increase overhead costs for the channel, right? Who do you think the company will pass on these costs to? Well, the consumer, isn't it?

Whichever way you choose to look at it, costs are bound to go up for cord cutters and video gamers as lack of Net Neutrality Rules will hand over control of data flow entirely and rather discriminately to operators. Therefore, Net Neutrality is critical to keep Internet costs affordable for the common man.

Net Neutrality Allows Equal Access to the Internet – Right now, everyone can access all kinds of content and data without having to worry about interference from Internet service providers and operators. These companies have nothing to say about what content is accessed by who and when. But, if Net Neutrality is lost, ISPs could begin to dictate terms to their users as to what kind of content they can watch or what they cannot.

The ISPs will be legally free to extort users to pay more to access social media sites even though they are not bandwidth guzzlers like video streaming services. The control of the flow of data will be in the hands of your ISP. If the ISP wants you to be a more Google Duo User than a Skype user, it will simply need to block out or throttle Google while increasing speed of Skype. Therefore, access to the Internet will not be equal anymore. It will depend on what your ISP is offering and what you can afford to buy.

Net Neutrality creates a level-playing field for all content and websites leaving you as the user in control of what you want to access. Yes, there are controls for illegal and other regulatory requirements. But other than that, your ISP is legally bound to give you access to the entire Internet without discrimination towards one or other content. AT&T or Comcast cannot decide how and what content the customers want to be delivered. This simply means that customer can choose to access everything from the Internet at the same speed and ISPs cannot give preference to one or more channels or sites or content types or applications, etc.

Net Neutrality is Good for Freedom of Expression – It fights against censorship. A non-neutral Internet will not lead to suppression of freedom of expression because operators will be powerful enough to throttle them either by increasing costs or by decreasing speeds or by blocking content leaving you tied to only those content that your ISP chooses to send your way.

Moreover, Net Neutrality will empower ISPs to suppress individual sites and what they are trying to say to the world. While until now, we have found the potential for bigger players like Netflix and Amazon Prime to lose out because of Net Neutrality, it is going to have a far more impactful effect on smaller players and the minority groups as they stand to lose the only open and truly unbiased available to them, the Internet.

Without Net Neutrality, ISPs could choose to completely shut out small voices that are until now depending on the Internet for support and help. The Internet is a pure bastion of free speech. With Net Neutrality being taken away, a few players could decide to alter or even cut down the powerful tones of free speech that is the fundamental basis of a democratic world. Lack of Net Neutrality could give unprecedented and disturbing controls to existing large corporations and majorities leaving out the progress of the weaker and minority sections at the back.

Net Neutrality Serves the Purpose of Innovation – Today, there are many companies which are billion-dollar enterprises; for example, Facebook, Google, etc. All these billion-dollar companies were at one point in time a little startup. One of the primary reasons the founders of these companies were able to not just survive but also thrive in this competitive world is the availability of the Internet access without discrimination which is nothing but Net Neutrality.

Net Neutrality ensures the same access to data to big companies as well as mid-size and small-sized companies. Everyone can survive and thrive because they get treated on an equal footing. Getting access to and uploading information and data from and to the Internet is completely free from discriminating between small, medium, and big companies which allows innovation to take place freely and uninhibitedly.

Only when startups have it easy can innovation take place. If they have to struggle to even access data from the Internet how will the next Google or Facebook or Amazon come into being? Without innovation, how will human beings progress? Net Neutrality is a key element in keeping the innovative spirit of human beings alive and kicking.

Net Neutrality Allows for ISPs to be Treated as Utility Companies – Just like how utility companies are strictly monitored to ensure regulatory compliance so that they cannot hold consumers for ransom, if Net Neutrality exists, ISPs can also be treated as Utilities and can be strictly monitored for misuse of their power. Today, without any doubt, Internet access is as important as access to water and drainage and therefore, needs to be classified as essential services. Utilities are regulated to deliver services to everyone equally unless there is a default in payment from the consumer. If ISPs can be treated as Utilities, then they will also have to deliver the same level of service to everyone without discrimination.

Cons of Net Neutrality

Advantages and disadvantages are simply a matter of perspective. If a mother looks on her eldest with more love than her second child, it is a disadvantage from the perspective of the latter and an advantage from the perspective of the former. It is up to the mother to ensure balanced outlook so that each child feels safe and equally well-looked after. That is what governments, policies, and systems are for; to give succor and comfort to all stakeholders while by balancing the entire system. And this is a continuous process that needs constant monitoring and supervision. Let us look from another perspective and view the cons of Net Neutrality.

Net Neutrality Makes it Tough for Internet Service Providers – The largest hit taken due to the effects of Net Neutrality is the group of ISPs or Internet Service Providers. Large companies like Comcast and Time Warner Cable have spent a lot of capital to lay cables and put up the necessary equipment all across the globe so that you can access the Internet from the comforts of your home.

In addition to the establishment and setting up costs, these companies are also spending money for the upkeep and maintenance of these large systems. Moreover, all these entities expect profit too as they do not run charitable organizations using voluntary donations to run their business. They expect returns on their investments.

Their cost is proportionate to bandwidth usage. The more you use, the more their cost rises. Net Neutrality prevents them increasing charges proportionally. While some of the ISPs have passed on the difference of charges to bandwidth-guzzling companies such as Netflix and others, their hands will be irrevocably tied if Net Neutrality policies get stricter than they already are.

Net Neutrality Compels Low Bandwidth to Subsidize Costs of High Bandwidth Users – For example, let us consider a grandmother who is using her Internet only to send a weekly email to her children and another young boy who uses the Internet to play highly interactive and bandwidth-guzzling video game. If you look at their charges, both of them are paying the same amounts. Is this fair? Why should the old grandmother (using extremely low bandwidth) subsidize the Internet costs of people who are high bandwidth users? Net Neutrality drives this scenario as ISPs are not allowed to charge differently for different users.

Therefore, Net Neutrality makes enormous data be used without any compensation being paid for that usage. Someone ends up paying for someone else's usage. Moreover, legal and illegal video streaming services are treated on par for the ISP and there is no way the company can manage to control the costs of legal services because the illegal ones are using up so much of data without any compensation due to the existence of Net Neutrality. If Net Neutrality continues to exist and/or gets stricter than it already is, then the ISPs will have no say in this and they will not be able to fix the system such that everyone pays only for what he or she gets or uses.

Net Neutrality Could Reduce Addition of New and Innovative Infrastructure – If income from their business slows down or is not even incentivized enough, it is possible for many ISPs to leave out innovation out of their systems and growth trajectories. With Net Neutrality limitations removed, high bandwidth users can be made to pay charges in proportion to their usage resulting in added income to the ISPs which can be used for improving infrastructure for better Internet experience for the users. After all, profits are what drive and keep innovation alive.

Just like ISPs believe that Net Neutrality is making them spend unreasonably and want it repealed, the consumers also believe that Net Neutrality is saving them money and why should they worry about the ISP's profits. These conflicts between the service providers and end users are bound to reach a deadlock resulting in slowing growth and development of ISP infrastructure which is going to hurt the end user finally.

For this point, however, there are counterarguments from the proponents of Net Neutrality as they believe that broadband infrastructure should compulsorily be supported with government funding and grants. Therefore, the capitalist-minded people say Net Neutrality will kill innovation in broadband infrastructure while the more left-leaning people say the government needs to increase investment for broadband infrastructure development (which is again taxpayer money, isn't it?)

Questionable and Dubious Content Could Flourish – Offensive, questionable, and dubious content may not just survive but also could end up flourishing on the Internet if Net Neutrality becomes stricter than its present form. These types of content include those that are offensive or critical of personal and/or religious beliefs and faiths. It could also include graphic videos, legal pornography, and other such content that are not suitable for children. While there are tools available for parents to filter out such content from their homes, opponents of Net Neutrality Rule use this point to argue that such content can be completely eliminated at the ISP level itself so that even the survival of such objectionable websites and content can be nipped in the bud.

Increased Governmental Regulations and Control Can Potentially Slow Down Everything – The founders of the US government also thought like this. The founders of this great nation believed that the biggest danger to the people of the newly born country is to lose the morals and ethics of the people to fast-paced and incomprehensible growth. They, therefore, deliberately made the government framework to work slowly and inefficiently by having multiple regulations. The same effect will take place if unnecessary and undue regulations are put in place. They will hamper growth and development.

Public Utility Companies have their Own Problems – Many utilities are facing problems of shrinking consumer base due to lack of innovation. This is resulting in increased

29

costs to existing customers. Therefore, customers are paying more for the same services without any innovation or growth, whatsoever. Treating ISPs as utility companies can result in a similar situation.

The debates of pros and cons of the Net Neutrality will continue as both sides have strong points and arguments in favor of their perspective. It is important, therefore, to take the perspectives of all stakeholders before coming to any decision that could prove one-sided and unfair to either side.

Chapter Four: Internet of Things and Net Neutrality

Let us start this chapter with understanding the meaning of 'Internet of Things.' When the world of computers and, subsequently, the Internet started its journey, human beings typed in all the data by typing out data or keying in information or scanning images or recording the voice of a speaker or anything else that needed human work to be done.

As we advanced in computing technology, we realized that the speed of human work is highly limited and cannot be easily scaled to very high levels. Moreover, data capturing in real time was not really possible if humans had to intervene. Not having access to real-time data would have resulted in taking wrong decisions or badly timed decisions that were either too early or late for worthy implementation.

That is when Internet of Things (IoT) came in handy. The 'thing' in the 'Internet of Things' could be anything ranging from the data in a pacemaker to a microchip implanted in a wild animal for monitoring purposes or anything else that can be given an IP addressed and connected to other devices via the Internet. The availability of Net Neutrality is crucial for the Internet of Things to thrive as partial or preferred treatment could take us back a few years resulting in collecting erroneous and/or slow data.

With more and more people using a lot of connected devices, the Internet of Things is becoming better ingrained into our lives. From voice-controlled virtual assistants to thermostats in cars and homes to lighting and heating in your home, everything in the world can be interconnected through the Internet of Things.

Although the impact may not be immediate or direct, Net Neutrality could have slow but long-lasting effects on the IoT. For example, as of now, the IoT devices are more or less connected within private networks. Yet over time, with loss of Net Neutrality Rules, ISPs could have reason to interfere even with these private networks and create blocks and throttles.

Today, the Internet of Things might appear frivolous, insecure, or not developed enough to worry about too much. It is after all in the nascent stage of development. But what we need to understand is the IoT is set to change the way we live in this world. IoT is set to help us save water, save electricity, enhance crop yields, and more. While big players are still to come up in this niche, a potentially bright future exists for it. It is still like a spoonful of data being sent as against drums of data by large players.

Yet, loss of Net Neutrality Rule could impact these interconnected devices potentially resulting unprecedented problems. For example, Comcast, a leading global ISP, could partner with a specific company to build and develop smoke detectors and if you are a member of Comcast in a world without Net Neutrality, you could, in effect, be left with no choice but to invest in the same smoke detector for optimal effect. Let us look at how the Internet of Things will be affected by loss of Net Neutrality.

Throttling and Blocking of Internet Traffic

Larger companies dealing with Internet of Things might still get off the hook if they are willing to shell out huge costs to keep their data in the 'fast lane' or 'preferential treatment' mode. However, smaller companies (and startups) that offer smart home technology solutions could get hit as ISPs can choose to throttle and block traffic from their IP addresses.

Data carriers and operators can potentially block and throttle traffic based on their own discretion without thought to long-term social or user benefits. Of course, it could work differently if the required price is paid. However, there could be instances in which ISPs could get into partnerships with specific smart home solutions providers and ensure only their data get preferential treatment while data from and to the IP addresses of competition is blocked or throttled. This could result in a non-competitive kind of monopoly in the industry which could potentially be harmful to consumers in the long run.

While such plans definitely don't seem to be in the offing for any ISP, there is no guarantee that such a thing will not take place in the future. After all, which business entity will deny more profits than before? Moreover, every business is under tremendous pressure to constantly improve their bottom lines. Isn't that what a hardcore capitalist is trained to do?

Negative Impacts on Small Businesses and Enterprise Users

While I must endeavor to place on record that taking advantage of any new rule immediately on its implementation (the elimination of Net Neutrality in this case) is highly unlikely, history teaches us plenty of lessons wherein small companies and businesses have been wiped out due to changes in regulatory policies. The same situation holds good here too.

But take this scenario. An ISP could easily tell GE, a large company dealing in IoT business, that unless GE pays a premium for data transfer via the Internet, the ISP cannot guarantee delivery of the required level of service. GE could still take on the pay hike and pass on the charges to its large base of customers who will not have much of a choice to do anything else except pay the difference in pricing.

However, imagine the state of a startup in the IoT realm. Would it be financially equipped to pay the hike? Even if it agreed and, like GE, decided to pass on the cost to its small base of customers, will they be willing to pay? It is highly likely that customers will move out from the services of the startup and go to GE as they will more easily be willing to pay a big player the same amount in return for assured guarantee of services that a small player may not be able to provide.

You cannot really blame the customer for making this choice. After all, he wants value for money spent and if the small company will not guarantee service, then he is bound to move to a bigger player who will give him the required guarantee. But that small business will sooner than later go out of business because of this draconian increase in pricing because of the removal of Net Neutrality Rule.

The Internet of Things industry like most other Internet-based industry thrives on the free flow of data via the Internet. If this free flow is stopped for any reason, the industry is likely to suffer damages and the entities in the industry are bound to feel the negative impacts soon. Again, it may take time and something new might come up to keep the small businesses still running. But taking stock of impending risks is a wise thing to do in any business, especially the small ones which run on very small profit margins.

Chapter Five: Big Data, Artificial Intelligence, and Net Neutrality

What is big data and artificial intelligence? Let us start from that and then move on to understanding how Net Neutrality or the lack thereof will affect the two emerging and growing elements of the technological world.

Big Data

Eric Schmidt, Google's Executive Chairman, said that from the time humankind started a civilization on this planet until the beginning of 2003, we collected about a total of 5 Exabyte's of information. Today, the human world through its technological devices and through the data produces the same amount every two days. That is Big Data.

The above statement clearly gives you an indication of the rate at which the amount of data being generated is moving. Millions of mobile phones and mobile devices generate data in seconds, Facebook and other social media platforms generate a humungous amount of content and data per hour and every business enterprise and every business sector produce new information every millisecond.

Big Data represents the running and management of large corporate houses that manage large volumes of data using massive infrastructure that is both cloud-based and on their premises. The Big Data phenomenon has led to new challenges for organizations during processing of such information. These challenges include collecting, transforming, storing, analyzing, and finally safely archiving it with easy retrieval access. Every aspect of managing big data has both opportunities and challenges to overcome. Some of the huge challenges these Big Data companies face include:

Big IT Resources and Infrastructure – Any company using Big Data technology will invariably have to include a very high variable workload in which there is huge consumption of rigid technical infrastructure, plenty of storage, and large amounts of bandwidth. To be able to even set up a Big Data company, it should invest in implementing the latest technology to manage and handle large volumes of data on a consistent basis.

Software and Applications – Big Data companies need complex and a variety of software applications to process, analyze, and create meaningful data to serve customers. Plenty of other technological tools must continuously be scaled and/or added to existing application platforms to a build a reliable and stable data environment to enable consistent and quality customer services, to increase profits, and make innovative business decisions.

Fragmented Data – This is another huge challenge for Big Data companies wherein different types of information are stored in different ways and at different places. Every section of the business invariably will hold its own data in different forms. This 'fragmented form of data' makes it very difficult for the company to integrate all of them in a meaningful way. Moreover, the quality of data can also be affected because information from one section could affect the data and outcome of another section. Each section is independent and no one section is responsible to collect and organize all the data in a cohesive and meaningful form.

Competent and Skilled Human Resources – Finding the people with the right set of skills is a challenge in any industry and more so, in the Big Data segment considering the fact that it is still in a nascent stage of development. People need to know how to work on and with data analytics solutions and cull data that is presented in a meaningful way such that it can be used to drive business and deliver customer service.

Big Data and Net Neutrality – Now that the challenges are clear to you and you understand how difficult it is to run a Big Data company, you must realize the additional pain of having to deal with the loss of Net Neutrality too. Net Neutrality is the basis for the smooth functioning of any Big Data company. Let's looks at a few examples of how Big Data companies could be negatively impacted by loss of Net Neutrality.

The Taxi Industry – Until the emergence of Uber and other lesser known taxi services, the taxi industry was one that lacked transparency, had poorly behaved drivers, badly maintained cars, etc. Of course, like in most places, there were people who did a great job in the taxi industry. Yet, there were more the exception than the norm. Today, with companies such as Uber, the taxi industry has undergone changes tremendously and customers are offered amazing, accurate, and disciplined taxi service from and to nearly every nook and corner of the world.

All this was possible because Uber's system was able to collect, analyze, create, and productively use meaningful data to deliver the services to their customers. The fact that Net Neutrality is available simplifies Uber's Big Data processing capabilities. Now, with Net Neutrality removed, what if a major ISP decided to block or throttle data flow to and from Uber's systems or even slowed down speeds to less than optimal.

Without the power and fairness of Net Neutrality, the chances of people giving up on Uber apps are very high (if the ISP chooses to play dirty) and we could relegate back to the old badly maintained system or find a monopoly in the market that is in connivance with the ISP leading to exorbitant pricing with or without innovation.

Let us look at another company that manages Big Data applications quite heavily; Tesla. This highly innovative company is developing ways and means to let the car systems talk to each other in such a way that users can predict and proactively do maintenance work on the vehicle's software and hardware. These new approaches are being developed by using huge amounts of data that is collected from its cars and vehicles and analyzing and creating solutions with the analyzed data.

If Net Neutrality is lost and companies like Tesla cannot communicate with all its vehicles and collect crucial data, how can such Big Data information find value for improvement of human life? Moreover, the enthusiasm to play around with Big Data and find interesting and meaningful solutions by analyzing the large volumes of information will be lost by even companies that are more than happy to invest profits towards research and development for improved products.

Thus, the most important thing for making Big Data Analytics useful and meaningful is the availability of a free, open, and non-discriminatory information highway which is what the Internet is today with the power of Net Neutrality in place. Free and open data flow is essential for crucial data to be captured correctly, accurately, and in a timely fashion which can then be used to analyze, understand, and use in ways that can help in both creating new solutions and improving existing solutions.

Net Neutrality is critical for the creation and growth of a healthy competition that will emerge on a fair playing field.

Artificial Intelligence (AI)

It is important to spend a little bit of time on what is Artificial Intelligence to even begin to understand how badly loss of Net Neutrality can affect this emerging and highly promising technology. Since the beginning of the invention of computers, human beings have been and are continuously working on improving and bettering their capability to do tasks given to them.

Humans have developing computers with exponentially increasing speeds of processing and ones that are slicker, slimmer, and more compact than ever. Artificial Intelligence is a branch of Computer Science in which people are working on creating machines that can be as intelligent and smart as human beings.

John McCarthy, the father of Artificial Intelligence, said this of AI: 'It is the science of computing in which we create and engineer intelligent machines and intelligent computer programs.' AI is a way of making a computer or a robot (that is controlled by a computer) or any software application that works and thinks intelligently, just like how we humans do.

AI can be successful by studying and recreating the processes that our brains use to think and work, the way we learn and understand things, and the way we solve problems. The AI engineers and scientists are studying these processes of human beings and recreating the processes within computing devices and applications.

The basic philosophy of Artificial Intelligence is the fact that as humans we are always trying to push our limits and in the same line, we want to know if it is possible for machines and computers to behave like human beings. Therefore, the goals of Artificial Intelligence are:

1. To create expert systems which can learn new things, exhibit its learning through demonstrations, explain what it has learned, and even give advice and suggestions to the users.

2. To get machines to be intelligent like humans so that these machines can learn, think, and behave like human beings

Artificial Intelligence is a science that combines the theories and practices of multiple other sciences including:

- Computer Science

- Biology
- Psychology
- Linguistics
- Mathematics
- Engineering

Why is Artificial Intelligence Important? To answer this question, the first thing to do is compare programming with and without AI. So, here go the comparisons.

- A program or application without Artificial Intelligence can only answer questions which have been posed to it whereas an application or program with AI can answer all generic questions that were meant to be solved.
- Any change in the application or program without AI will require appropriate changes in its structure whereas one with Artificial Intelligence can simply absorb new changes and modifications by putting together information appropriately on its own. Therefore, the structure of the system with AI need not be changed to make any alterations to the program.
- Any modification or change is not easy and the outcome could negatively impact the program (without AI) itself. A program with AI, on the other hand, can be easily changed or modified without problems.

In the world of humans, knowledge has multiple limitations including:

- The volume of knowledge is unimaginably huge
- Human knowledge is neither well-formatted nor well-organized
- Knowledge is constantly changing

AI is created to overcome these exact problems. The purpose of AI is to use this vast amount of knowledge in a way that is:

- Perceivable by the users
- Easily modifiable (especially useful to correct errors)
- Useful in multiple situations even if the knowledge is not accurate or complete

Where is Artificial Intelligence Used? There are various industries where Artificial Intelligence is dominating and some of them include:

Gaming – AI plays a very important role in developing and improving mental and strategic games such as poker, chess, tic-tac-toe, etc where machines are made to think of many different possibilities of moves and positions based on historic knowledge.

NLP (Natural Language Processing) – Machines and computers empowered with Artificial Intelligence are able to interact with people even when they are speaking in any human language. AI in this realm is able to learn and respond using natural languages spoken by humans.

Speech Recognition – Some machines are intelligent enough to hear and understand the language by comprehending the sentences and phrases used by the people talking to it. Such machines can handle a lot of dialects, slang, accents, and background noise as well giving you accurate results.

Expert Systems – There are computer applications that combine software skills, machine skills, and other special skills to reason out, explain things, and give advice to users.

Handwriting Recognition – There are multiple software applications that can read and understand your writing (done through a stylus, usually) on the monitor and convert the content into editable text.

Vision Systems – These systems are able to see and understand visual input given through the computer. Here are some examples of vision systems embedded with Artificial Intelligence:

- Face Recognition – Police and detectives use this software to match faces and facial features with those on their database and identify unknown people who could be witnesses, suspects, etc in a crime.
- Drones and Spying Devices – These devices can scan an area and take photographs which can be used to check out spatial information of the areas.
- Diagnosing Devices – Doctors use these AI-powered devices to help in diagnosing the patient's problems

Robots – These are entities that can do tasks just like humans do. They have sensors all over that are capable of detecting and comprehending the effects of physical senses like touch, movement, etc and using that data to do things just like we would.

AI and Net Neutrality

Considering the wide range of applications for Artificial Intelligence, it is no surprise that people associated with this system of computing are keen on keeping the Net Neutrality on hold. The concept of one or two entities controlling the entire Internet ecosystem is scary to people who take innovation and research seriously. And Artificial Intelligence is the ideal example of innovation that is happening in the computer world.

Moreover, Artificial Intelligence is being combined with Internet of Things and creating even more useful and wonderful solutions and products for humankind. IoT will bring in an enormous amount of devices onto the Internet and by combining AI solutions and creating new and innovative interface systems, more powerful and meaningful solutions could emerge in the future. Experts from MIT believe that AI can deliver amazing value but slowly if we can connect our refrigerators, our thermostats, our home lighting systems, etc on to the Internet and effectively to each other.

Again, the key element for the success of such systems is Net Neutrality. If data cannot pass through the various systems and get choked and throttled by ISPs, there is a huge danger of our losing steam in AI and IoT segments. The computer is here to stay in the human world and it would be naïve to try and control the way it is moving forward. We can only try and keep pace with the movement and not relegate our progress back by a few hundred years simply because a few thought that Net Neutrality is not good for us.

Chapter Six: Questions of Ethics Surrounding Net Neutrality

In addition to many drawbacks that have been discussed in this book already, loss of Net Neutrality could potentially create a new kind of net-based divide or 'caste system' in the world. There was a time when the divide was created between the people who had access to the Internet and those who didn't have access to the Internet.

Even today, there are many parts of the world where Internet access is not available as freely and with the same speeds as those available in developed countries. These Internet have-nots are created because of socio-economic divide and such divisions can be taken care of through help from both the non-governmental and governmental organizations committed to scale up people in remote and less-than-average societies.

However, when Net Neutrality is brought into the picture or rather removed from the picture, even if some charitable organization finds the means to give Wi-Fi connections and laptops to these have-nots, they may not be able to access the Internet. The divide or gap could continue to exist. With the lack of Net Neutrality, these people could very well not have access to the 'complete' Internet or could have access at extremely low speeds making the Internet experience bad enough not to want to go back there again.

Ethical Players in the Net Neutrality Debate under Utilitarianism

There are three primary players in the Net Neutrality Debate in the US and they are:

1. The FCC that make the rules and governing policies

2. The consumers who form the largest group of players in this debate and they stand to lose or gain a lot from the outcomes of this debate

3. The ISPs or the Internet Service Providers who may be much smaller in number but form the sturdy and absolutely essential pillars of the Internet ecosystem

The FCC – already explained in an arm of the government responsible for overseeing the communications department including the computing world and the Internet. This group consists of lawmakers, scientists, and other experts who are responsible for listening to all sides of a debate and then take appropriate action for the greater good of the nation and its people.

The Consumers – Consumers are the largest set of people to be hugely affected by changes in the Net Neutrality policy. Consumers in a free world expect to have control over what they can access from and see on the Internet. This freedom of choice is the most basic foundation based on which the Internet was invented/discovered. Consumers expect Net Neutrality policies to:

- Protect consumer liberation
- Preserve freedom of expression and speech by ensuring that all content is treated equally without discrimination

47

- Prevent the wide world web to be managed and controlled like the telecom segment that is overly regulated
- Promote healthy competition and innovation on the Internet

The ISPs – The Providers are like pillars holding the entire Internet up for use by everyone in the world. These entities have invested large amounts of money on creating great infrastructure making it possible for the Internet to reach nearly every nook and corner of this wide world.

They own the backbone of the entire Internet framework and therefore (even if slightly unpleasantly for certain sections of societies like the activists, etc), are well within their rights to ask for more rights and controls on how to manage the backbone they use. Of course, this means they want access to manage those parts of the Internet framework that are not directly connected to the backbone they created. For the ISPs, extant Net Neutrality policies:

- Are not conducive to network infrastructure investments and development as they have lesser control over economic outcomes and the way businesses can be modeled for optimum benefit
- Encourage equality even in the way data is managed and controlled even in essential services which is as non-humanitarian as it can get; for example, they argue that if a fire service needs to have priority of data over someone who is playing a game, they are unable to do this presently because of the strict Net Neutrality Rule
- Discourage innovations as increased regulations will simply lead to an environment that holds on needlessly to archaic ideas which have no value

More from the Perspective of the ISPs

Being a highly polarizing topic, Net Neutrality, more often than not, takes very dramatic turns and is also presented dramatically. Nothing works better for a polarizing topic than drama, I suppose. The villains in this debate are the telecom companies, the ISPs, and the cable operators while the good guys are the scrappy business newbies that have little or no resources to set up companies and depend solely on the Internet to build and grow their passion. This is what the entire scene will appear as from the perspective of the ISPs.

Many times, the good guys are also amazing content providers and video application owners such as Netflix or Google or Skype which deliver content 'over the top' of the Internet network because of their huge bandwidth requirements. Such companies have, therefore, been named as 'OTTs.'

Let us accept certain things in the debate of Net Neutrality. Stakes are huge and the future of Internet hangs by a thin thread. Well, this is a simple scenario that is presented by proponents of Net Neutrality. Well, the ISPs opine that this is a very simple story that tells a complicated tale.

The ISPs believe that some realities are lost in the big drama of the hero v/s villain. Today, from a drama perspective, the OTTs seem to be winning the hearts of the common man while the ISPs are simply relegated to the position of bad, greedy guys who need to be beaten up. Here are some of those realities about OTTs:

- Google's market cap is more than that of 4 ISPs put together
- The five top Internet companies make up for more than 60% of the traffic across the United States
- The Internet is not really dominated by scrappy startups but by some of the richest companies on earth
- Many of these OTTs do not require the protection of the government anymore

Here is a second thing that is being left out of the debate by the 'heroes' to the Net Neutrality cause. Innovation needs a robust and fast network to move ahead in the right direction in today's highly competitive world. It is true that innovation could be in the form of a spectacular service or app that changes the way the world works. This amazing service needs to be hand-delivered to every device and system through the network only.

If there is a lag in the network or if it fails, the services and apps supported by the network also fail. That means, this great free Internet can be active only when the transmitting network is robust and excellent working condition. The unfortunate thing about the network is that is largely invisible to the common man. Yet, there is no doubt that a faulty network can create hell for the end users. They are an essential part of a smooth and interactive Internet experience. Moreover, our dependence on network companies is increasing day by day.

Be it cloud computing or driverless cars or virtual reality or big data or artificial intelligence or any new innovative technology that is being created and/or will be created, a powerful network is a must for their success. In fact, the development of each new app or service or technological advancement simply deepens our dependence on a well-framed and well-structured broadband infrastructure that can be easily scaled to higher capacities depending on the need of the service or app.

A third concern is being understated in the drama debate, say the opponents of Net Neutrality. This is the concern of the huge bandwidth requirements of video content. There is a deluge of videos being produced and shared across the Internet resulting in unprecedented pressure on the existing network. In fact, the pressure from delivering seamless video content is so huge that ISPs will not be able to deliver in a way that the proponents of Net Neutrality are fighting so hard for.

The amount of video content is only increasing and there is no way this is going to subside as more and more people are discovering the interactive and engaging power of a video. To this already overflowing deluge, add Augmented Reality, AI, and Internet of Things and you can only imagine the huge delivery pressures that the existing broadband technologies are going to face sooner than later. All these humungous amounts of information and data that is flowing through the Internet are putting more and more pressure on the pipes and other infrastructure.

Looking at it in this perspective, it looks like the bigger threat to innovation is the lack of sufficiently scalable broadband infrastructure as compared to Net Neutrality or the availability of completely free and open Internet even to those who don't need or want it. ISPs will have to invest a lot create the right kind of infrastructure that is needed to support and meet the expectations of the next generation of apps and services and content. Yet, they claim, the current way of doing business is resulting in most of their revenue being channelized to meet the subsidies of OTTs that are bandwidth guzzlers who are unreasonably protected by Net Neutrality.

A Few Answers to a few Questions on Ethics

Here are some questions that can be posed to check the ethics and legality of Net Neutrality.

Q1. Should a business entity discriminate against the content being transmitted across the Internet?

A1. Legal experts agree that while there are no laws in place to make cutting lines or queues illegal. But it is not an ethical thing to do. Yes, it is true that there are no criminal or civil penalties that can be levied on people who choose to break a line that is formed to get a service. However, there is no doubt that it is unethical to do this. What will happen is the people who are waiting in line (quietly and seemingly submissively) and those who do not have alternative queues to join will be disenfranchised or even cheated of their expectations.

The ISPs' power to be able to prioritize one set of contents over another (if Net Neutrality becomes a thing of the past), many Internet users are going to feel the same way as those who waited in line and were overtaken by those who didn't have to wait in line. Therefore, if content to these people was blocked, choked, or interfered with in any way, they will be left with no recourse if they want only general service. They might be compelled to take on prioritized service at a premium even if they didn't need to.

You can easily see that this is a clear case of abuse of freedom that comes from unethical behavior and as a civilized set of people, it makes sense to avoid it even if the profits seem irresistibly attractive.

Q2. Since the Internet from the time of its invention has been a platform for freedom and innovation without undue political influence, shouldn't it be treated as a public utility?

A2. A public utility company is a business enterprise participating in essential public service while being regulated by federal and/or state laws. Yet, it was an exception to the utility monopoly regulation that gave us the Internet. In this circumstance, it might appear that governmental control over it is unethical. But, it would be equally (if not more) unethical of any corporate practice of selective controlling of content considering the fact that the Internet was and is meant to be free and open to one and all.

Let us look at the FCC at this stage. The FCC or the Federal Communications Commission is a government agency overseeing the computing world (as part of the overall communications segment) in the US. Being part of the government, it can be hugely influenced and powerful lobbying by telecom, broadcast, and information providers to get regulations passed that are suitable for their own businesses. The influence of this one particular federal body is powerful enough to break or make companies and/or individuals.

Giving powers to the FCC that has the potential to imperil the freedom and openness of the Internet could prove dangerous. The 'Great Firewall of China' is definitely what comes to mind as an extreme case of over-enthusiastic regulatory control over the presently free and open Internet.

Ethical Test of the Net Neutrality Based on Utilitarianism

Under utilitarianism, any course of action is considered ethical if it provides greatest good for the greatest number of people. An act is considered ethical if the total benefits can be maximized without regarding burden or distribution. The basis of Utilitarianism is utility. Since any federal government is responsible for the overall good of the entire nation, it makes sense to consider the ethics of Net Neutrality based on Utilitarianism.

So, to summarize, while consumers want to have freedom and control over data without being discriminated against, the ISPs argument of increasing cost is valid too. How does one balance the cost while being fair to the greatest number and yet, keeping the power to innovate and get improved products and solutions? It is indeed an ethically complex question.

Utilitarianism Test Conclusions

Utilitarianism works on the premise of greatest good for greatest number. The consumers form the masses and will definitely benefit from the equality and freedom of Net Neutrality. ISPs are critical and have their own concerns, many of them quite valid and in need of redress. If the FCC sides with Net Neutrality, it is on the side of the consumers in the short-term but could end up being on the opposite in the long-term. So, we must ready ourselves for more debate and more discussions on this highly complex and difficult subject before reaching any decision.

Conclusion

There is no doubt that Net Neutrality debate is not just complex but very polarizing owing to the fact that there are multiple businesses, multiple entities, and nearly the entire globe involved. The amazing amount of connectivity that the Internet offers has been highly beneficial to humankind.

- Consumers are empowered with unprecedented choices in terms of availability of a variety of products and solutions.

- All users are able to access and understand varying viewpoints, opinions, and standpoints leading to a potentially mature human race that can perceive and sympathize with differing opinions and cultures and way of life followed by people all across the world.

- Content Owners and Service Providers are empowered to develop new and innovative products and services that consumers can lap up making them rich and happy. The market base for content owners and service providers is limitless with the availability of the Internet.

Everyone is benefitted from the Internet and now comes the crux of having to reach a solution that is a win-win for all. So, this concluding chapter has a few recommendations on how the Net Neutrality debate can be solved amicably.

Some Recommendations to Address Dilemmas of the Net Neutrality Debate

Experts, activists, and stakeholders are in constant dialogue with each other trying to solve this rather befuddling issue.

Here are some recommendations that have come up in the course of discussions and debates:

- If ISPs are truly concerned about delivering content with discrimination except for a good cause, they must be willing to make voluntary public pledges or sign contracts stating that they will not engage or indulge in abusive behavior. These kinds of public pledges and demonstration of signed contracts will go a long way to keep consumer fears at bay.

Moreover, when such deeply embedded fears in the minds of the consumer are addressed openly and transparently, they will be able to take informed choices about such controversial matters. When fear based on lack of knowledge or lack of confidence is addressed, consumers are sure to understand and appreciate the concerns of the ISPs and will be happy to pay a little more for long-term benefits such as innovation and development.

Even though there haven't been any case of abusive behavior driven by a lack of Net Neutrality yet, the degrees to which such potential abuses can reach is making the stomachs of consumers churn in discomfort which is bound to exhort activists and other affected people to enhance their fight against dropping Net Neutrality. However, open, bold, and transparent moves such as voluntary public pledges and/or signed contracts that bind ISPs to being fair and non-abusive will drive down the heat in this fight which could result in a win-win situation for all.

- While the government may have participated a little in the formation of the Internet, it is only without its direct control that the Internet has been able to flourish the way it has and the way it can potentially do in the future as well. Those who want to keep utility-like controls on the Internet must think of important things such as the absolute need for freedom to exist to maintain and grow the vibrancy of the Internet.

  While control can easily taken away, the giving up is far more difficult. The FCC is an arm of the government headed by only one government appointee and therefore, in no democratic way reflective of the people's will. Such a lot of controlling power needs to be and will be scrutinized just like or, perhaps, more than many private players. As rules change and as restrictions and endorsements alter, more and more political mileage can be misused resulting in unpleasantly partisan ways.

- The FCC is the go-between between the two sides of the debate; the consumers and the ISPs. It is imperative, therefore, that they keep the public clearly informed of all the happenings, the deliberations, the outcomes of deliberations, etc. Yes, the common citizens use the Internet in a huge way. Yet, there are many in this group who are not aware of its history, of its way of working, of the varied layers of architecture, the subtleties that can be controlled so well that no one will know who is the actual controller, etc.

  In addition to appointed politicians, elected politicians should also treat this issue with caution before making their opinions public. They, after all, represent the public and it is imperative that they understand all aspects of this complex issue in a mature manner before making their opinions and stance public. Misrepresented talks and skewed opinions are bound to spread more ignorance among the masses resulting in more pain in solving the already contentious issue amicably.

- From the consumer's perspective, it is our duty to learn and educate ourselves about this issue before standing on one or the other side just for the sake of debate. It is important to read more about this controversial subject, understand where the controversy is coming from, and make an informed choice of whose side you want to be in. We are, after all, huge beneficiaries of this amazing technology. It is our duty to learn about its history, its way of functioning, how it operates, who are the stakeholders, what are their roles, and why is there such a big stir in this debate?

Then, armed with all the necessary information, you can take an objective stand and speak to people about it in an open and fair manner. Look at it from different angles and participate in various discussion forums. Talk with your neighbors, colleagues, etc. See if you can contact your local government representative and talk to him or her and see where things are moving.

If you are an expert in the field, do not hesitate to put your ideas and opinions online through articles, guest posts, etc so that more and more people become aware of Net Neutrality in a deeply involved way and not merely scratch the surface and arrive at some skewed decision. The more awareness that is created, the better will be the outcome of this controversial debate.

Therefore, it is for all of us to sit together, plug the loopholes on each of our sides, bring forth all the cards to the negotiating table, and arrive at a solution that is beneficial for everyone.

Resources

https://www.savetheInternet.com/net-neutrality-what-you-need-know-now

https://www.Internetsociety.org/policybriefs/networkneutrality/?gclid=EAIaIQobChMI75ibif2V2AIVyiMrCh2tKAyoEAAYASAAEgICqPD_BwE

https://www.ofcom.org.uk/consultations-and-statements/category-1/net-neutrality

http://www.newsweek.com/net-neutrality-money-facebook-twitter-720279

https://vittana.org/13-pros-and-cons-of-net-neutrality

https://cordcutting.com/the-pros-and-cons-of-net-neutrality/,

https://www.wired.com/2017/06/end-net-neutrality-shackle-Internet-things/

https://www.networkworld.com/article/3238016/Internet/will-the-end-of-net-neutrality-crush-the-Internet-of-things.html

http://www.itprotoday.com/Internet-things-iot/will-dismantling-net-neutrality-affect-iot

https://www.networkcomputing.com/applications/why-net-neutrality-matters-big-data-apps/642268115

https://cyberscience365.physics.lsa.umich.edu/f17/2017/12/12/what-net-neutrality-means-for-big-data/

https://www.tutorialspoint.com/artificial_intelligence/artificial_intelligence_overview.htm

http://www.ancapbarbershop.com/net-neutrality-artifical-intelligence-abs019/

https://www.theguardian.com/technology/2015/oct/14/government-regulation-Internet-of-things

http://www.sanduskyregister.com/story/201411160034
https://thehumanist.com/magazine/november-december-
2010/up-front/net-neutrality-google-and-Internet-ethics
https://uconnbusinessethics.wordpress.com/2015/02/13/is-
net-neutrality-ethical-from-a-utilitarian-framework/
https://www.youtube.com/watch?v=t-
zMoDVs5Ts&list=WL&index=8
http://fortune.com/2017/04/26/net-neutrality-trump/
https://www.ofcom.org.uk/consultations-and-
statements/category-1/net-neutrality

Made in the USA
Middletown, DE
21 March 2019